# Fun with Sorting

Katie Peters

GRL Consultant, Diane Craig,
Certified Literacy Specialist

Lerner Publications ◆ Minneapolis

**Note from a GRL Consultant**
This Pull Ahead leveled book has been carefully designed for beginning readers. A team of guided reading literacy experts has reviewed and leveled the book to ensure readers pull ahead and experience success.

Lerner Publications
An imprint of Lerner Publishing Group, Inc.
241 First Avenue North
Minneapolis, MN 55401 USA

For reading levels and more information, look up this title at www.lernerbooks.com.

Main body text set in Memphis Pro 24/39
Typeface provided by Linotype.

Photo Acknowledgments
The images in this book are used with the permission of: © tonephoto/Shutterstock Images, p. 3; © Elena Abrosimova/iStockphoto, pp. 4–5; © Mumin/iStockphoto, pp. 6–7, 16 (right); © Andrey Znamenskyi/iStockphoto, pp. 8–9; © Eleonora_os/iStockphoto, pp. 10–11, 16 (left); © Dasha Petrenko/Adobe Stock, pp. 12–13; © Dasha Petrenko/Shutterstock Images, pp. 14–15, 16 (center).

Front Cover: © Antonia Giroux/Shutterstock Images

**Library of Congress Cataloging-in-Publication Data**

Names: Peters, Katie, author.
Title: Fun with sorting / written by Katie Peters.
Description: Minneapolis, MN, USA : Lerner Publications Company, an imprint of Lerner Publishing Group, Inc., [2024] | Series: Math all around. Pull ahead readers - nonfiction | Includes index. | Audience: Ages 4–7 | Audience: Grades K–1 | Summary: "How would you sort your toys? By color, by size, by shape? Young readers will enjoy learning how using this colorful text. Easy-to-read text makes sorting fun! Pairs with the fiction title Match the Socks"—Provided by publisher.
Identifiers: LCCN 2023002428 (print) | LCCN 2023002429 (ebook) | ISBN 9798765608692 (lib. bdg.) | ISBN 9798765616307 (epub)
Subjects: LCSH: Set theory—Juvenile literature.
Classification: LCC QA248 .P388 2024 (print) | LCC QA248 (ebook) | DDC 511.3/2—dc23/eng20230712

LC record available at https://lccn.loc.gov/2023002428
LC ebook record available at https://lccn.loc.gov/2023002429

Manufactured in the United States of America
1 – CG – 12/15/23

# Table of Contents

# Fun with Sorting

You can sort by color.

I sort the rings. I put
the same colors together.

You can sort by shape.

I sort the blocks. I put
the same shapes together.

You can sort by size.

I sort the boots. I put the same sizes together.

# Did You See It?

blocks

boots

rings

# Index